DEALING WITH DIFFICULT PEOPLE

Smart Tactics for Overcoming the Problem People in Your Life

By
Robert S. Smith

Table of contents

Chapter 1: DEALING WITH DIFFICULT PEOPLE

We've all had to deal with them. Whether at work, at home, or at church, if you're around people long enough, you will eventually come across someone who is tough.
It's exactly as a friend of mine once remarked, "Pastoring would be the simplest job in the world if it wasn't for the people."

So what should we do when we meet someone who's difficult?
In church, we normally avoid this sort of disagreement. Whether it's in the name of being polite or giving grace, the fact is we're really poor at managing disagreement in the Body of Christ.

But we don't have to be.

We find in the Bible that Jesus did not shy away from conflict. He overturned tables in the temple (John 2:15-16), dubbed judgmental religious people "whitewashed tombs" (Matthew 23:27), and he even scolded one of his own when Peter chopped off the servant's ear in the Garden of Gethsemane (John 18:10-11). (John 18:10–11).

And since Jesus didn't shy away from tough individuals, neither should we. Here are four strategies for coping with the unpleasant individuals in your life.

Get Started Fixing It, and Start With You

One of my favorite sayings applicable in these situations is: "Control the knobs on your side of the wall." You can't control other people. You can only control your reaction to it.

For starters, speak to the individual, not about them. As a pastor, I talk all the time with folks who are trying to get along with someone else. They're typically glad to chat about how annoying the other person is. But when I ask, "Have you told them how you feel?" the response is generally no.

Next, be honest about how you've contributed to the problem. Maybe your colleague appears unhappy about a request you've made, yet your request was made at the last minute. Now they have to abandon everything to assist. Admitting your fault in the problem to yourself and others goes a long way toward restoring harmony.

It's not all about you.
Your husband comes home in a terrible mood because of an incident at work. But you take their sulky demeanor as aimed at you directly and respond by assaulting them.

What they actually needed was for you to assume the best of them, and gently ask if they wanted to chat about why they're having a poor day. This provides them the choice of talking about it (not everyone wants to process it vocally right away) and the ability to explain why they're not alright.

At work, your coworkers might be coping with any variety of personal concerns that impair their professional performance. Leading with compassion may de-escalate tension and provide you with the chance to express God's love to someone who may be in tremendous need.

Build Bridges
It may be as easy as finding out where they went to college, or their favorite team, or where they grew up...
In an attempt to find some tiny way to establish a bridge with the tough individuals in your life,

Be careful to listen intently and offer questions like, "What was it like to grow up in such a tiny town?"
Building bridges might sometimes mean you have to open yourself.

Have the guts to be honest about what you actually need from them. My coworker is off on maternity leave, and I'm having a terrible time obtaining responses from anybody on this project. Could you help? "

With your partner, establishing bridges may be as easy as working backward to get to the spot where you both agree on things. "We both agree we want to be prudent financially, right? So let's commit to utilizing our tax refund in a manner that helps us accomplish our long-term goals. "

Be kind.

I know it might be challenging, but even when someone is being harsh and unpleasant, reply with compassion. Have the strength to reply to a harsh statement with tenderness and tolerance. Think carefully before sending that nasty email to a coworker.
Stay cool when your partner disappoints you or damages your emotions.

You don't have to avoid a confrontation in these instances, but don't allow your sentiments to force you to begin with hostility.
Proverbs 16:24: "Kind words are like honey, delicious to the spirit and nourishing for the body."
One Final Thought: One of the easiest ways to keep on the right track in dealing with difficult people is to realize that, on some level, you are difficult people. (It's alright, I am too.)

Somewhere in your life, someone found you
hard to work with. At times in your marriage,
you've been the issue. It's hard to acknowledge,
but it's true nevertheless.
If you can recall all the times people have had to
show you grace and understanding, it will go a
long way to helping you discover the grace and
understanding to offer to others.

Chapter 2: COMMUNICATING WITH DIFFICULT PEOPLE

At the beginning of my company, I had a sales call with a highly dominant CEO. He revealed to me that on his sales team, 13 out of 16 weren't reaching quota. I joked with him that he had too many low performers on his sales team because he had "nice-guy syndrome." He stared at me and replied, "You have no clue what you're talking about."

Whoops! I was simply fooling around. He didn't appreciate it.
I am not sure how this transaction was rescued, but he did become a customer. We have a wonderful connection and we laugh a lot-but on his terms!

It took me a long time to grasp that you never laugh with a high-dominant person or attempt to charm them (hear that high I's?!?) while they are in go-mode. If you do, you are likely to be leveled.

I also learnt to "bottom-line" my message, leaving out my oh-so-entertaining tales and remarks. Once I accomplished this, my relationships with most high dominators appeared to improve.
It turns out that each DISC behavioral type has specific demands that we can address in our interactions with them.And when we unwittingly violate what they require, everything grinds to a standstill!

On the other hand, every DISC behavioral type also includes specific characteristics that may present a difficulty for us when interacting with them.
So what is the best strategy to approach them? That is what you will uncover via this series of articles.

However, no matter what DISC type you're working with, there are certain universal strategies for communication that work with each individual, no matter their style.

Tips for Communicating with Anyone
Talk it out or act it out? Your genuine sentiments are transmitted not only via your words but also through your body language, facial expressions, and tone of voice. According to research, when these elements are incongruent, your words only account for 7% of the information transmitted.

Control yourself! With each conversation, the only person you control is yourself. So there is no use in spending energy on attempting to alter the other person (as great as it might be) (as nice as that would be). As a result, when speaking with others, you must assume complete accountability.It is your behavior towards them and the talk that will decide the result much more than the conversation itself.

Assume the best. Orient yourself to this person's favorable characteristics. Every DISC style has its benefits and flaws. So if you're challenged by someone's shortcomings, they must have matching qualities.
C'mon-you can find anything if you search hard enough! Find something you appreciate and respect in this person and approach your next discussion with these traits in mind.

Analyze the facts vs. your opinion. This is where we typically get into difficulty. So... separate the facts from your emotions. What did you see or hear? Anything that gets put into "observable behavior" is typically your interpretation of the facts and will be different from how other individuals view the same occurrence.

Forget the Golden Rule. One of the precepts of all major faiths is a variant of the Golden Rule: "Do unto others as you would have them do unto you." This may be a good philosophy to follow with general acts of kindness, but it may be the

kiss of death when it comes to communication.
Why?

Because it's all about YOU! Communicating
with others the way you prefer to be
communicated with works for you, not always
for them.
What should we do when the other person wants
us to embrace them, yet their conduct is simply
plain wrong?

In today's fast-paced world, when most people
are more likely to be glancing at their phones
than making eye contact, merely pausing,
listening, and seeing—actually seeing—is a
gesture that goes a long way. People need to be
acknowledged and understood, and they are truly
moved when they discover that someone is
attempting to see and hear them, to give them
their attention.
Listening is pastoral care, and you can do it.
Listening is not simply a question of hearing
words; it is also about taking in the full person
and what he says and doesn't say, or in the

sentiments that cross his face or the gestures and movements of his body.

Occasionally, communication is more body-language based, and sometimes it occurs in utter silence. It's an art not just to hear but also to listen, taking into consideration the depth of communication and complexity of individuals and their past.

Control your negative emotional reactions.
It's not easy to comprehend people, particularly when they let go with intense sentiments, crazy acts, and harsh words. It requires significant effort and self-awareness to be able to welcome and understand someone even when their conduct is inappropriate, unintelligible, or harmful.

Sincere friendship is something on this planet more treasured than anything else.
We may require time, effort, and commitment to work on ourselves so that the initial wave of

emotions may settle down enough for us to obtain a clearer understanding of the problem.

 We should not act on heightened emotions or allow our sensations to be detrimental. Make time for yourself so that you can regain your equilibrium and calm.
Accept the person, not necessarily their behavior.
It's one thing to understand and accept the person... but it's another to accept and agree with their behavior. The two do not usually go together. We can understand and accept the person in all of his originality, uniqueness, and complexity without accepting or condemning all of his actions and choices.

A firm foundation of understanding helps us to voice differences in such a manner that the other

person does not feel rejected. We all need someone we trust, someone we can accept when they tell us, "I love you and I understand why you did this, but I disagree with it."
A Heart to Hear the Fear: The Mercy of Understanding

Give it time and stay present.
Learning to be in relationships may take a lifetime, beginning with the struggle in infancy to describe and comprehend emotions. As we continue to develop, we will make errors, and occasionally we'll be harmed by others' blunders. It is crucial not to wall oneself off and to hide from people.

 (Note: establishing protective boundaries against an abusive individual is a distinct topic.)

For well-intentioned individuals who battle with their own difficulties, emotions, and blunders, that continual open door is a reminder that our love and understanding are deeper than their good or poor decisions. It's a reminder that no matter what they've done, they're seen, understood, and loved—and that if they ever do want to change, someone is there to offer them a hand.

Chapter 3: DEALING WITH IMPOSSIBLE PEOPLE

Most individuals know someone who appears to make every situation poisonous and difficult. Pointing out that these individuals are tough and demanding won't get you far since they likely don't perceive an issue. Whether the problem is driven by a personality condition or some other underlying issue, you may learn how to negotiate relationships with difficult people and retain your own sanity.

Part 1.
HANDLING CONFLICTS

Don't become defensive. Stay cool, and be aware that you will never win an argument with an impossible person—they are referred to as "impossible" for a reason. In the impossible person's view, you are the issue, and nothing you say can persuade the person to see your side of the story. They believe that your viewpoint doesn't matter since you are guilty, whatever.

- Think through what you are going to say before you say it and what your purpose for the discussion is. Don't simply respond hastily because the other person angered you. You don't have to justify yourself to this individual.

Use "I" statements instead of "you" ones. For example, don't remark, "You are mistaken." Try something like, "I feel that that remark may not be the complete truth." This lets you voice your opinion without putting people on the defensive.

Detach, dissociate, and defuse. Keeping cool in the heat of the moment is crucial to your personal preservation. Spitting harsh words and responding with severe emotions such as sobbing, would only push impossible individuals to perform more of the difficult conduct. Don't take the responses of impossible people personally, and don't allow yourself to get emotionally heated in reaction to them.

- Remove yourself emotionally from the
  matter, and handle it with apathy. The idea
  is to not allow yourself to become
  emotionally engaged in the conversation,
  keep the person at a distance, and not let
  the words make you feel awful.

Redirect the situation or discussion to something
good by concentrating on something other than
what the debate originated over. Talk about the
weather, fishing, the difficult person's
family—really anything that will divert from the
disagreement and is not likely to provoke
additional conflict.

Consider the reality that whatever you do or say
when angry may be used against you. Unless
you don't mind hearing about an angry statement
years from now, let it go. Impossible people
want you to say anything to establish that you're
a terrible person.

- Do not evaluate this individual as right or wrong, even if they appear unreasonable. Judging is likely to simply make you feel worse.

  Avoid fighting with them. If possible, don't disagree with impossible individuals. Find ways to be pleasant or ignore them. Arguing will simply get you emotionally immersed in the issue and stimulate your fight or flight instincts. This will make it tougher for you to think clearly and react correctly. [1] Impossible people want a fight, so when you agree with them or find some truth in their argument, you are no longer giving them what they want.If you are branded a "jerk," for example, go ahead and recognize a time when you behaved improperly.

- This corrects an overgeneralization. Realize you probably can't have a rational discourse. Having a decent discussion with the impossible person is unlikely—at least with you.

Remember the last time you attempted to have a decent conversation about your relationship with the individual. You were probably blamed for everything instead.

When possible, use silence or try to amuse the individual. You know that you cannot "fix" impossible individuals. These folks cannot and do not listen to reason.

- Avoid being trapped in an argument. Don't deal with the individual one-on-one. I always recommend that a third party be brought in. If the individual refuses, demand it.

Ignore them. Impossible people crave attention, so once they realize you won't give them what they want, they will go on to someone else who will respond to them. Stay out of their business, out of their way and avoid talking to or about them.

Impossible people's tantrums are like a child's tantrum. Pay them no notice until the outbursts become disruptive, harmful, or menacing.

Do your best to avoid angering impossible individuals or giving them a chance to lose their temper.
It's best to simply keep away from poisonous individuals, if you can.

- Ask a thought-provoking question. Asking the impossible person or the group you are working with a question addressing the situation, such as, "What is the problem?" or "Why do you feel this way?" might be useful. It demonstrates that you are interested in the talk and eager to uncover the basis of the dispute. Rephrasing the impossible person's argument to reveal irrationality might inspire an individual to arrive at a better conclusion.

Know that the impossible person may reply to the inquiry by trying to complicate matters with

name-calling, blaming, shifting the topic or other
actions.

Take a breather. If the person you're chatting
with is getting on your last nerve, then you need
to walk away from the present scenario. They
could only try to get a rise out of you, so show
them that they have no influence on you.
Walking away or doing another activity so you
can cool down is a smart option.

Count to 10 quietly if you need to.
If the individual is still being difficult, then
simply ignore him. That individual will
ultimately back off if he discovers that he's not
irritating you.

- Be confident. State your thoughts with
  confidence and look the individual in the
  eye while conversing with them. One of
  these folks will not take you at your word.
  If you glance at the ground or over their

shoulder, she might see this as weak. You want to be reasonable but not timid. Adjust your approach. Sometimes you can't flee the circumstance, so treat it like a game. Learn the difficult person's plan, and build counter tactics ahead of time.

Eventually you'll uncover what works and what doesn't, plus you'll probably feel better as you know you're three steps ahead, outwitting them at every turn. Just remember that your ultimate objective is to assist liberate yourself psychologically, not become the person's master.

- If the impossible person comes up to you and whispers something unpleasant among others, believing you won't want to reply and cause a disturbance, then say out loud, "Do you really want to speak about this here?" This may startle them and deter them from exhibiting hostility to a whole group.

Always examine the probable implications of your actions if your plan doesn't go as intended, so you can prepare for them, too.

If the impossible individual still finds a way to get to you, then don't feel terrible. Just make a note of what occurred and design fresh techniques for next time.

Impossible individuals aren't so impossible when you can foresee what the person is going to say or do next.

- Check your body language. Become conscious of your placement, how you move, and your facial expressions while with these folks. We convey a lot of our feelings non-verbally. You don't want to betray your own sentiments accidentally. Also, this will help you maintain your own sense of calm and may have a calming effect on the impossible person in the process.

You may practice mindfulness to become more aware of your body, which will help you to check your body language more readily. Speak gently and move as calmly as possible.

Try a method called "slow speaking." By slowing your conversational pace by 1/3, you will sound clearer and calmer. You may practice slow speaking by reading aloud at an intentionally slow speed.

Avoid confrontational body language, such as eye contact for lengthy periods of time, hostile gestures, pointing or standing immediately in front of the individual face-to-face. Keep a neutral look on your face, don't shake your head, and keep out of the person's personal space.

Part 2

ACCEPTING THE SITUATION

Consider that there could be a concern about compatibility. Even though a person appears to get along with everyone else, they might be a difficult person for you. Some individuals just clash or don't get along well. There may be nothing wrong with either of you, but together you simply bring out the worst in each other.

- When an impossible person makes a remark like, "Everyone else loves me," they are attempting to transfer the burden onto you. How they connect with others is unimportant as there is an issue with the way the two of you interact. Remember that blaming does not change the facts.

Avoid taking on "impossible" qualities.

You tend to pick up on the conduct of individuals around you. For this reason, you might find yourself embracing the precise features that you despise by mistake. In response to the impossible person, you may engage in the same deceptive and unreasonable behavior.Catch yourself when you start to do this, and make a concerted effort not to emulate the offensive features.

- Avoid Caring About What People Say. Consider what you can learn. Impossible individuals bring great life experiences. After dealing with impossible individuals, you will be able to get along with most other people easily.

Try to preserve perspective and remember that what may appear strange to you may be another person's only method of survival. Try to consider these encounters as a means to cultivate traits such as flexibility, grace, and tolerance.

Never be deceived by a person's age, IQ, or position in life when judging her maturity level.

- Understand Your Emotions.

Be prepared for intense mood swings. If you successfully persuade an impossible person that they made a mistake, then they may suddenly have an emotional collapse. Instead of thinking they are right all the time, they will determine that if they can't be right now, then they will always be wrong. This is a coping method to solicit compassion from others.

Some impossible people may engage in unpredictable behavior in order to surprise and perplex others.It's conceivable they didn't even anticipate it either. Resist the impulse to let this type of unexpected conduct overwhelm you.

- Don't allow these individuals to fool you by pretending that they are being persecuted. If they truly feel awful for what they did, reply favorably, but don't

give them an incentive to manipulate you in this way.
Dealing With Impossible People Focus on the good.

Many individuals have some redeeming features, so try to think of anything. There could be something the person does well, or maybe there was a moment you were able to connect with her. If you can't think of anything good, then create a statement for yourself like, "All life is sacred" or "God/The Universe loves her" to help keep yourself under control—even if you don't love or appreciate them personally.

• Date a Man Who Has Children
Talk to someone. If you know someone who will be understanding of the circumstance (good friend, family, counselor, etc.), speak to that person about it. They would probably understand you, and it would surely make you feel better. It is better if the listener doesn't know the impossible person personally and is not engaged

in the same settings (for example, not a
co-worker).

Vent in a diary or online community if you need
to.
Sharing your feelings, whether with another
person or in a diary, can help you avoid
obsessing over negative emotions.

Part 3
PROTECTING YOURSELF

Cope With Feelings of Love for the Wrong
Person at the WrongTime Preserve your
self-esteem. Maintaining a good self-image in
the face of someone who presents you as a nasty
person requires work. Instead of listening to
what the difficult person says, concentrate on the
people who affirm you and make you feel good.
Realize that the impossible person wants to harm
you to make themselves feel better.

- Understand that the impossible person is the problem—not you. This may be challenging since impossible individuals are adept at transferring the blame and making you feel like it is your fault. But if you accept responsibility for your faults and weaknesses and endeavor to better yourself, there's a very strong probability that you are not the impossible person.

When somebody makes a comment aimed at harming you, know that all they want is for others to think that they're amazing. You know, you don't need affirmation like that.

If the insults have no foundation in truth, simply reject them. You are not as horrible as that impossible person would want you and everyone else to think.

- Get Your Friend to Leave His Girlfriend

Maintain your privacy.Impossible individuals will frequently find ways to use your personal information, even if it appears trivial and tiny, against you. They may make up entire stories about you and portray you as a bad person based on a single statement you made. As professionals in manipulation, impossible people are also quite skilled at persuading you to open up and tell them stuff.

- Don't tell impossible individuals anything personal, even if they look normal or seem like a friend to you at times. Things you say or share in confidence might suddenly come back to haunt you unexpectedly in your personal or professional life.

Get Over Your Depression
Be the antithesis of them. Be a "possible" person—make yourself and your life an example of tolerance, patience, humility, and compassion. Always attempt to be the rational one. Consider all sides of the story before coming to conclusions.

Just as poor conduct may impact us adversely, acting like a tolerant, patient, and kind person can occasionally influence someone for the better.

Recognize that you aren't flawless. You don't have to do everything perfectly all the time, but do your best. Be respectful, and if you don't get respect in return, then recognize that it's the other person's issue and not yours. You will have good days and terrible days, just as with everything else in your life.

- Deal With Your Friend's Boyfriend Hitting on You

Don't concentrate on them. Even if you cannot avoid impossible individuals in your everyday life, don't worry about them in your "off" time.

Remember that fretting over the individual all the time is the same as giving them your valuable time when they don't even care about you. Do other hobbies and establish new acquaintances; that way you aren't wasting time by worrying about what the individual said or did continually.

Turn your thoughts to what you do want in your life, rather than what you don't want. This helps you stay focused on the good instead of the bad.

- Dealing With Impossible People You should know that you may be dealing with an emotional abuser. Emotional abusers may cripple you with their words and deeds. They utilize strategies like humiliation, denying, criticizing, dominating, accusing, demanding, and emotional distance to make you codependent on them. Never allow what emotional abusers say to define who you are. Know that the things they say and do are from unresolved childhood or previous problems that they are transferring onto you.

The best thing to do is to be pleasant and friendly, even if the impossible person may behave like a jerk to attract negative attention. If the individual feels lonely but doesn't know how to gain attention, then they will appreciate what you are doing and change.

If the individual is simply a natural jerk who likes to make people upset, then what you are doing will infuriate the person since they can't figure out how to make you furious. Eventually, the individual will leave you alone.
In certain situations, a person who shows these traits is a sociopath.

A sociopath may first appear quite charming, but they eventually become dominating, abusive, and narcissistic. Since they lack empathy, they don't care about you.

- Helping Loved Ones with Histrionic Personality Disorder

Set limits. Declare the ground rules for what is and is not acceptable in the relationship.Determine that neither of you will bring up particular themes, events, people, or act in a specific manner. [8] It may be useful to sit down with the impossible individual and let them know what is and is not appropriate and what will happen if limits are breached.

 Allow them to make the decision to obey the rules or not.
Write down some ideas and make a mental note of your wants and needs.Sit down with the individual and start conversing. If they interrupt, stop them and continue your discourse until you are done. Be honest. Give ultimatums if you must, but stress the advantages of remaining and altering the negative behavior.

- If you decide to continue a personal connection with an impossible individual, then keep to yourself as much as possible. Find and concentrate on a hobby, join a support group, or focus on your faith.

Make sure to follow up with repercussions if boundaries are broken. Don't let anything slip. If you stated you'd be out the door, then out you go.

Heal from Emotional Abuse. part ways. Eventually, you will need to remove yourself from an impossible individual. Even if they are a family member, you will probably need to leave at some point. A long-term relationship with an impossible individual is not healthy. Remove the individual from your life as soon as you can.

- Stay away from the person when you leave. No matter how much you love the person or if they attempt to persuade you that they have changed, don't go back.

If you can't leave or make the impossible person go right now, then leave the relationship psychologically until you can do it physically. Severing your relationship with an impossible person can be painful in the beginning but will be liberating once you can move past old habits.

Part 4
DEALING WITH PERSONALITY TYPES

Be a Cynic Try to find out what irritates you about the individual. We all have some characteristics of our personality that others can characterize in a few words. Some individuals are clinging, domineering, playing the victim, passive-aggressive, excessively theatrical or highly competitive.

 If you can articulate what it is about the impossible person's personality that conflicts with yours, you may be able to discover particular approaches to cope with him. Clinging types are insecure and might be yearning for attention and love since they feel weak and admire stronger individuals.

- Controlling types are frequently critical perfectionists who need to be correct and often blame others for their actions.

Competitive types usually want to win and frequently use any form of relationship, discussion or activity as a contest to show they're superior at anything.

Passive-aggressive persons exhibit their animosity indirectly by quietly pressing other people's buttons. An example is the remark, "Don't worry about me, I'm OK," when you know that if you carry on with whatever you were doing, there will be difficulties to deal with later.

- Know what doesn't work. Some things work better for some sorts of individuals, while others won't. It may take some trial and error to find out what is and is not going to work with the impossible individual. It is also likely that there is nothing you can do to make dealing with her easier most of the time.

Avoiding clingy types will simply make them strive harder. However, rejecting them publicly might turn them into an adversary. If you stay distant, then their sentiments are wounded.

For a controlling type, you can't establish that you are right and they are wrong. They always have to be right no matter what, and performing a better job won't help get critical perfectionists off your back.

People that are highly competitive will use what they regard as weakness against you, so don't exhibit emotion around them. If you stand up to them and strive to win, then they tend to either forsake you or never let it go.

Don't agree with complainers or attempt to soothe them. They'll simply become outraged over something else.

Victims want you to feel sorry for them. Don't express pity, and don't let them make excuses either. Be realistic and offer to assist in other ways.

- Find out what works. You may work with particular personality types to assist cope with the bad parts. Use their abilities to help solve disputes and relationships stress and minimize flaws. Dealing with certain people this manner may create extremely favorable effects.

Deal with clinging, domineering and competitive sports. Understand why some sorts of individuals behave the way they do. People who are clinging require leadership and responsibilities to help them build confidence. Those who are domineering are frequently insecure and fearful of their own shortcomings. Competitive sorts of individuals worry a lot about their self-image, thus they can generally be quite pleasant and giving once they win.

- Show clingy types how to accomplish things and then let them figure it out. Don't allow them to attempt to persuade you that they shouldn't try anything because you would do better. Seek out instances when you need aid and ask them.

Don't be afraid or allow what dominating types say to get to you. Acknowledge when you do a good job but don't dispute with them if they suggest differently.

You can simply let competitive people win. If you are having a disagreement they won't back down, recognize their perspective and ask for time to conduct further research.

- Deal with self-important individuals, complainers or victims. Understand that self-important individuals only need to feel like others are listening to them. Somebody who complains a lot frequently has a lot of internalized anger from unsolved situations, and often also requires people to listen. Those who play the victim usually have terrible things happen to them so that they have an

explanation for why they haven't accomplished anything.
If you're dealing with a self-important individual, then simply hear them out.
Put up with individuals who whine a lot, recognize how they feel and try to get away as much as possible.
Overlook the reason victims are late or making trouble and behave as you typically would to someone else without an explanation. You can provide counsel but don't become emotionally entangled.

- Deal with histrionic and passive-aggressive types. Histrionic personality types thrive for attention, and will usually go to tremendous measures in order to receive it. They have to live in the correct area, wear the proper clothing and send their kids to the appropriate schools. Passive-aggressive persons are typically unpleasant because they don't know how

to communicate their goals and
requirements effectively.

Regardless of sex or gender, histrionic persons
are commonly referred to as "drama queens".
Avoid getting caught up in the drama and
emotional rollercoaster these folks bring with
them. Listen but maintain your distance.
Deal with passive-aggressive folks by being
extremely explicit about the actions and
circumstances that may be a concern. Then try
resolving the issue by being non reactive to the
animosity. Set limits, and encourage the
individual to voice desires and needs as well as
how to ask for things assertively.

TIPS

If you believe that you may be an impossible
person, then you have already passed over the
first stage of acknowledging that you are being
impossible. Learn to examine other people's
perspectives with an open mind. Keep your own
views, but know that just because a viewpoint is
yours does not make it the correct one.
Stay cool and composed but do not use sarcasm
in dealing with unpleasant people at work. You
might perhaps lose your job or be reported so
strive to be professional.
Never resort to violence as a remedy.